D0375065

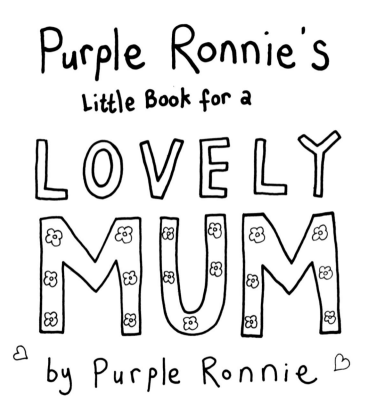

Purple Ronnie's

Little Book for a

LOVELY MUM

by Purple Ronnie

First published 2006 by Boxtree
an imprint of Pan Macmillan Ltd
Pan Macmillan, 20 New Wharf Road, London N1 9RR
Basingstoke and Oxford
Associated companies throughout the world
www.panmacmillan.com

ISBN-13: 978-0-7522-2564-7
ISBN-10: 0-7522-2564-2

9 8 7 6 5 4 3 2

A CIP catalogue record for this book is
available from the British Library.

Text by Giles Andreae
Illustrations by Janet Cronin
Printed by Proost, Belgium

Interesting Fact

Mums are absolute experts at doing hundreds of things all at the same time

Rules of Being a Mum - N°1

Once in a while, it's good just to really spoil yourself

Some mums are more than just mums—they're best friends as well

☆ **Special Tip**

Never trust a mum
whose kitchen is too tidy

Rules of Being a Mum - Nº 2

When you become a mum, you will not get a proper night's sleep for about 20 years

Pants

When you are a mum you are allowed to wear big pants even if your bottom is actually quite small

v.comfy

☆ Special Tip for Mums

Make sure your man is as well trained as possible

Rules of Being a Mum - Nº3

From now on, at least half of your life will be spent in the car

☆ Special Tip for Mums

Sometimes chocolate is very, very helpful indeed

There is nothing a mum loves more than a really good gossip with her friends

Rules of Being a Mum - Nº 4

Every year it gets more difficult to make your tummy look like it used to

Some mums find it hard to get dads away from watching the T.V.

☆ **Special Tip**

Try to make a bit of time for yourself every day to do what you want to do

Rules of Being a Mum - Nº 5

Your kitchen is a free restaurant and you are the cook, the waitress and the cleaner

Sometimes mums get worried that being a mum makes their brains turn to jelly

☆ Special Tip

Never tell a mum that you love her squidgey bits - even if you're trying to be nice

Rules of Being a Mum - Nº 6

Suddenly you see the point of shops you never used to understand

Sometimes, not even the fanciest restaurants can beat mum's home cooking

Mums love nothing more than looking at old photos of their little darlings

Rules of Being a Mum - Nº 7

Sometimes it's best just to let your man get on with it and try not to laugh

☆ Special Tip

Sometimes mums need a little bit of extra help to get them through the day

me feeling v. smug
oh, you're the loveliest son in the whole world!

☆ Special Tip

Give your mum a little treat once in a while and she will think you are amazing

Rules of Being a Mum - Nº 8

However much you try not to, sometimes you end up sounding exactly like your own mum

Sometimes mums have to have very long arms indeed

Some mums love nothing better than a really good session in the garden

Rules of Being a Mum · N° 9

You must be even better at settling arguments than a wrestling referee

☆ <u>Warning</u>

When you become a mum,
your shopping list
completely changes

Sometimes even mums
need a little bit of
peace and quiet

Rules of Being a Mum - N°10

However much a mum gets done in a day, there is always something more to do

Remember
_____

Most mums are really
angels in disguise